THE MANCHESTER SHIP CANAL

A Portrait in Old Photographs and Picture Postcards

by

Chris E Makepeace

G000057558

S. B. Publications

By the same author in this series: The Lost Villages of Manchester

First published in 1993 by S.B. Publications
c/o 19 Grove Road, Seaford, East Sussex BN25 1TP.

ISBN 1.85770.019.8

Printed and bound by Manchester Free Press
Longford Trading Estate, Thomas Street, Stretford, Manchester, M32 0JT

CONTENTS

CONTENTS

S.B. Publications

ACKNOWLEDGEMENTS

I am grateful to Steve Benz for suggesting this approach to the subject and, also, to Mrs Pam Brown for the loan of many of the postcards which have been used in this book. I must also thank my wife, Hilary, for her encouragement whilst working on the book, and Peter and Anna, who are always being told about the Ship Canal and its importance.

My thanks also to:

Gillian Jackson, for editing the text;

Steve Benz, for additional editing and marketing;

Manchester Ship Canal Co. for allowing the use of the coat of arms on page vi.

Cover photograph: Barton Bridge

INTRODUCTION

The centenary of the opening of the Manchester Ship Canal takes place in 1994. The completion of this major civil engineering project - a modern parallel of which might be said to be the construction of the Channel tunnel - enabled ocean-going vessels to reach within a couple of miles of the heart of one of England's major inland industrial cities and the centre of the Lancashire textile industry. It was the culmination of a dream which Mancunians had held for many years. The result of the opening of the Ship Canal was that importers and exporters no longer needed to rely on the railways and Liverpool docks but could use some of the most modern port facilities in the country.

This book is not the story of the construction of the Manchester Ship Canal; this has been written about at length and photographs of that work can be seen in my book *The Manchester Ship Canal*. Rather, it is a journey along the Canal as seen mainly through the eyes of the picture postcard. However, it has been necessary to use some other photographs to enable all the important locations to be recorded. I hope the result will be of interest to many people.

Chris E Makepeace,
Disley,
Cheshire.

THE MANCHESTER SHIP CANAL

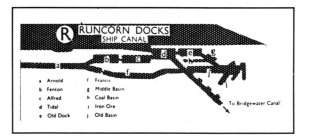

RUNCORN DOCKS
SHIP CANAL

a	Arnold	f	Francis
b	Fenton	g	Middle Basin
c	Alfred	h	Coal Basin
d	Tidal	i	Iron Ore
e	Old Dock	j	Old Basin

To Bridgewater Canal

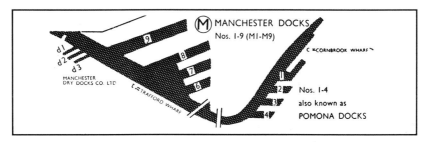

MANCHESTER DOCKS
Nos. 1-9 (M1-M9)

C CORNBROOK WHARF

MANCHESTER DRY DOCKS CO. LTD

E TRAFFORD WHARF

Nos. 1-4
also known as
POMONA DOCKS

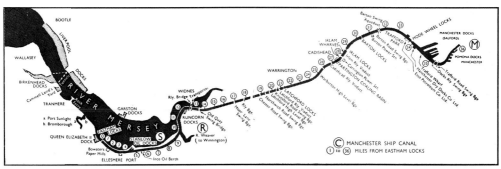

C MANCHESTER SHIP CANAL
1 to 36 MILES FROM EASTHAM LOCKS

vii

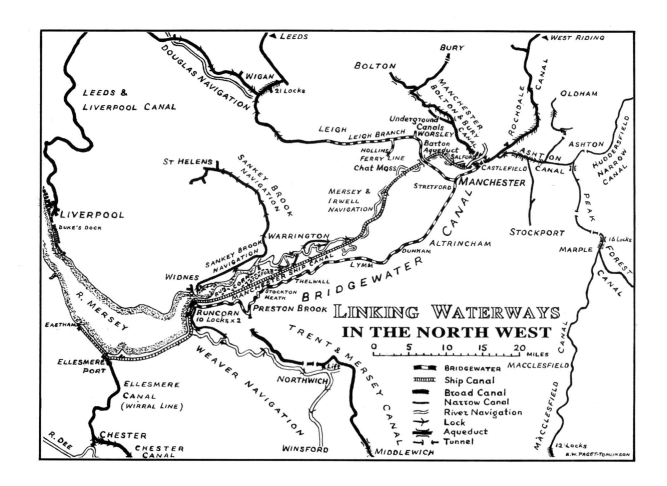

viii

MANCHESTER SHIP CANAL, c. 1904

The Act of Parliament which authorised the construction of the Manchester Ship Canal was passed in 1885 after a three year struggle against the vested interests which were opposed to it. Work started on 11th November, 1887 and, despite many problems, was completed in December, 1893. A section of the canal was partially opened for traffic in 1891, but it was not until 1st January, 1894 that it was opened for vessels wanting to reach Manchester. The official opening took place on 21st May, 1894 by Queen Victoria. The 35.5 miles long canal cost £15m and was able to take all but five of the ships that existed then. This view shows the Mode Wheel Locks looking towards Manchester.

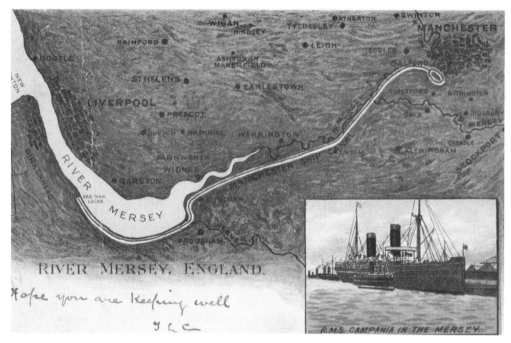

MAP OF CANAL, c. 1902

The Manchester Ship Canal closely follows the River Mersey between Eastham and Warrington. East of Warrington, between Bollin Point and Irlam, it crosses the River Mersey and follows the course of the River Irwell, until it reaches Manchester. This postcard shows the route of the canal together with some of the towns which were close to it and which benefited from its construction.

CANAL PIONEERS.

The driving force behind the movement to build the Ship Canal was Daniel Adamson, owner of an engineering works near Manchester. It was Adamson who called a meeting at his home, the Towers, Didsbury, Manchester, which resulted in the formation of a provisional committee which prepared the scheme and presented the bills to Parliament to authorise the canal's construction. Adamson resigned as Chairman in 1887 and died shortly afterwards. However, his contribution to the success of the project was marked by the inclusion of his portrait on this souvenir card. Others depicted included Leader Williams and Marshall Stevens, both connected with the construction of the canal.

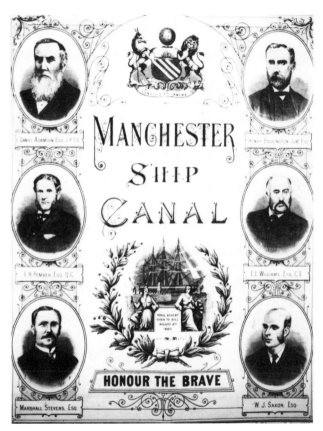

LORD EGERTON OF TATTON

Adamson's successor as Chairman of the Manchester Ship Canal Company was Lord Egerton of Tatton. He became chairman at a time when the Company was facing difficulties in raising the necessary finance for the project. His appointment restored confidence in the Company with the result that the sum of £5m, which was required before construction could commence, was raised by the end of July, 1887.

THOMAS WALKER

Another major figure in the project was the contractor, Thomas Walker. Walker had extensive civil engineering experience, his firm being involved in the construction of the Severn Tunnel for the Great Western Railway Co. He estimated that the work would be completed within 4½ years and cost £5.25m. Walker did not live to see the completion of the Manchester Ship Canal. His death in 1889 precipitated a major crisis as his executors were not prepared to allow the firm to continue with the work. Eventually, the Manchester Ship Canal Company took over the construction, but this required substantial financial assistance from Manchester City Council.

10718. PORT SUNLIGHT. THE WHARF – JUDGES'LTD

THE WHARF, PORT SUNLIGHT, c. 1920

Although not on the Manchester Ship Canal, those sailing to Eastham would have passed the works of Lever Brothers at Port Sunlight. At the beginning of the twentieth century, the works occupied some 20 acres. The main product was Sunlight Soap of which 1600 tons were produced each week. Employees of the firm were housed in a model village, opened by Gladstone in 1891, where the properties were built in the "Old English style". This postcard shows the soap works at Port Sunlight with the wharf and several barges in the foreground.

The Lock. Port Sunlight.

THE LOCK, PORT SUNLIGHT, c. 1908

A tidal channel connected the Lever Brothers Works at Port Sunlight to the River Mersey. Because it was tidal, the dock at the works was protected by a lock gate which enabled vessels to remain afloat and be loaded even when the tide was out. This postcard shows the entrance to this dock. Water was also used as a feature of the landscaping of the site by the firm.

EASTHAM PIER, c. 1907

Even before the construction of the Manchester Ship Canal, Eastham was a popular place with trippers from Liverpool. It was known as the 'Richmond of the Mersey' because of its beautiful countryside and Pleasure Gardens where there was entertainment for all the family: circus, fairground, animals, dancing and all sorts of variety acts. In the early 1890s, the journey by boat from St George's Landing Stage in Liverpool to Eastham took three-quarters of an hour and cost 4d for adults and 2d for children. This postcard shows two such pleasure-steamers at Eastham in 1907, some thirteen years after the Ship Canal was opened. The pier is situated just before the entrance to the Canal.

Eastham   *Ferry and Pier*

PASSENGERS LANDING AT EASTHAM PIER, c. 1902

Eastham Pier was constructed in 1874, by Messrs Thompson and Gough, to enable visitors to disembark at Eastham at all states of the tide. The pier, which cost £6000, allowed visitors to the area to avail themselves of country walks, a visit to the village of Eastham or the Ferry Hotel and Pleasure Gardens. Once work started on the Manchester Ship Canal, there were many visitors to the site. For example, at Easter 1892, 33,000 visitors went to Eastham to look at the progress of the works. The pier was demolished in 1935 but, in recent years, a short length has been constructed and this gives visitors a good vantage point for watching shipping on its way to and from the Canal.

EASTHAM LOCKS ENTRANCE TO PORT OF MANCHESTER SHIP CANAL. K539

AERIAL VIEW OF EASTHAM LOCKS, c. 1950
The Manchester Ship Canal at Eastham is approached along a specially deepened channel in the River Mersey.
This aerial view of the entrance to the canal clearly shows the three locks at Eastham, the relationship of the canal
to the river and the site where the Queen Elizabeth II oil dock was to be constructed later (bottom right).

GENERAL VIEW OF THE EASTHAM LOCKS CLEARED FOR THE ADMISSION OF THE WATER.

EASTHAM LOCKS CLEARED FOR THE ADMISSION OF WATER, 1891

Construction of the Manchester Ship Canal started officially at Eastham on 11th November, 1887 when the Chairman and directors cut the first sod. The land was handed over to the contractor in stages, when all the necessary equipment and men for a particular stage had been assembled. This postcard shows the locks before water was admitted on 2nd July, 1891. The first section of the canal to be used commercially went only as far as Ellesmere Port. It was a further twelve months before the next section, to Saltport, was ready to receive water and be used commercially.

EASTHAM LOCKS

There are five sets of locks on the Manchester Ship Canal: Eastham, Latchford, Irlam, Barton and Mode Wheel. The locks raise the canal 60 feet 6 inches from the Mersey Estuary to Manchester - most of the rise taking place between Latchford and Manchester. With the exception of Eastham, the locks are in pairs. The first set of locks is at Eastham. This undated view shows them shortly after the canal was opened. At this time, the railway type signals which advised ships when it was safe to enter or leave the lock, do not appear to have been installed.

EASTHAM LOCKS, c. 1908

This is the view which sailors approaching the entrance to the Manchester Ship Canal would have had in 1908. The central lock was used for the largest vessels whilst the smaller locks were used by smaller vessels, thus reducing the demand for water when the locks were operational. In the background can be seen Mount Manisty, named after the engineer responsible for this section of the canal. Mount Manisty consisted of spoil from the canal excavations which was used to form a barrier between the River Mersey and the Ship Canal.

EASTHAM LOCKS, c. 1921

At Eastham, there are three locks, the largest measuring 600 feet by 80 feet and the smaller ones 300 feet by 50 feet. The remaining locks are a little smaller, measuring 600 feet by 65 feet and 350 feet by 45 feet. The entrance cills were originally placed 28 feet below the surface so that the canal could be deepened without the need to close it and reconstruct the locks. This was a far-sighted decision as the canal was later dredged to a deeper level. The gates each weigh 500 tons and are made of greenheart, a very hard wood. At Eastham, the main lock gates were protected by additional gates to prevent damage by tidal action and storms. This view was taken from inside the locks. An M.S.C. tug is on the left.

EASTHAM LOCKS, c. 1930

This view of Eastham Locks was taken from the site of the Queen Elizabeth II Dock and is looking seaward. The central pier, between the locks and the sluice gates on the left, is 30 feet wide. It was calculated that it took between five and seven minutes for a vessel to pass through a lock, depending on the size of the ship.

EASTHAM LOCKS, c. 1913

A ship in Eastham lock waits for the signal to proceed on its journey. Note the lines holding the ship steady whilst the water either enters or is let out of the lock. At the stern of the ship, a tug also helps to hold the ship in position. This vessel is the *Andoni* and she appears to be carrying a cargo of timber.

EASTHAM LOCKS, c. 1913

A group of tugs awaiting their next job. Although it was not mandatory for ships to have tugs and pilots when travelling along the Ship Canal, many captains preferred to take advantage of these facilities. Several sections of the canal were difficult - especially where the River Mersey crossed the canal and in its narrower sections. This photograph was taken shortly after the one on the previous page. The *Andoni* is now proceeding into the canal accompanied by two M.S.C. tugs.

SAILING SHIP AT EASTHAM, c. 1905

When the Manchester Ship Canal was built, as many bridges as possible were constructed so as to be swung open, but those carrying railways had to be fixed. The minimum clearance for the fixed bridges was about 70 feet, but there were vessels whose masts and superstructure exceeded this height. In order that these vessels could reach Manchester, it was necessary to provide facilities to remove the tops of masts and funnels. These facilities were located close to Eastham Locks. The sailing ship appears to be unloading its cargo into a lighter alongside.

SAILING SHIPS AT EASTHAM, c. 1910

In order to ensure the maximum usage of the Manchester Ship Canal, it was important that time taken to travel along it was kept to a minimum. Therefore, the canal was constructed so as two vessels could pass each other at almost any point along the canal, except at locks. The average width of the canal at water level was 172 feet whilst on the bed it was 120 feet wide. This postcard shows not only the width of the canal but, also, a sailing ship moored at a jetty with Eastham locks in the background.

QUEEN ELIZABETH II DOCK, EASTHAM, c. 1955

As the demand for oil and petroleum increased, so also did the size of tankers which carried it. Aware that vessels larger than about 12,000 tons were not able to use the canal, the port authorities constructed a special dock at Eastham, just before the main Eastham lock, with its own lock 807 feet long and 100 feet wide, capable of taking tankers of up to 30,000 tons. The Queen Elizabeth II Dock is the largest enclosed dock in the United Kingdom, covering 19 acres, and was officially opened on 19th January, 1954. The tanker on the right of this view is the *Newbury*, (11,119 g.r.t.) built in 1951 and owned by the Houlder Line.

THE LIGHTHOUSE, ELLESMERE PORT, c. 1914

When the Ship Canal was completed Ellesmere Port had three wet docks which were said, in the 1890s, to have been 'well equipped with hydraulic cranes and other appliances'. None of these are visible on this postcard, but one feature that is associated with seafaring is - a lighthouse. Until the Manchester Ship Canal was completed, the only vessels which could reach Ellesmere Port from the River Mersey averaged 200 tons, with the largest being only 400 tons. This view shows one of the docks and a sailing ship tied up at the quayside. The warehouse is the Ellesmere Port Grain Elevator, constructed by the Manchester Ship Canal Company and completed in 1899. The lighthouse and adjoining office were built in c. 1802 and mark the old River Mersey entrance to the Shropshire Union Canal which now opens onto the Ship Canal. These buildings are still standing.

21

THE GRAVING DOCK, ELLESMERE PORT, c. 1905

Amongst the other facilities at Ellesmere Port was this graving dock, which could be emptied of water, to allow the hulls of vessels to be inspected, repaired or cleaned of barnacles. Although it would have been able to take only relatively small vessels, it would have provided an important service for ship owners. It was all part of the policy to make the canal as self-sufficient as possible and provide those using it with the best possible support services.

EP.39 MANCHESTER SHIP CANAL, ELLESMERE PORT

THE CANAL AT ELLESMERE PORT, c. 1960

This view was taken between Ellesmere Port and Stanlow. At this point, the River Mersey and the Manchester Ship Canal run very close to each other. In order to separate the two waterways, a mile long embankment was built, using material excavated during the construction of the canal. Part of this embankment can be seen on this postcard, which also shows the Shell-Mex & B.P. tanker *Shell Director* (891 g.r.t.), built in 1946. The Shell refinery and chemicals complex is just visible in the distance.

OIL DOCKS, STANLOW, c. 1935

Although described as 'Oil docks, Ellesmere Port', this postcard shows one of the two special oil docks at Stanlow - on the left. From here, the unloaded cargoes passed in a series of pipes beneath the canal to oil refineries - on the right. The Stanlow Oil Docks are capable of handling tankers up to 15,000 tons. In addition, there is also a lay-by which allowed vessels to discharge oil and also take on fuel oil for bunkering purposes.

STANLOW, c. 1950

At Stanlow, the Manchester Ship Canal Company constructed a special dock for the unloading of petroleum and other products which had a low flash point and which were, as a result, very dangerous. This special dock was constructed on an isolated part of the canal, next to the River Mersey so as to minimise the danger to other ships and property when such cargoes were being discharged. This aerial view shows the oil docks on the right of the illustration, and seen from the opposite direction to the view on the previous page. The oil docks are built on the site of Stanlow Abbey and some interesting artefacts were discovered when the docks were being excavated in the 1920s and 1930s. The ship in the centre is being guided by tugs towards Ellesmere Port and on to the River Mersey and the sea.

THE TUG *STANLOW*, c. 1930

This tug was named - like many others working on the Manchester Ship Canal - after places which the canal passed. This one was named *Stanlow* after the oil docks located there. She has the black and white striped funnel of the Manchester Ship Canal Company. Built in 1924, she was a 480 h.p., screw tug of 100 gross tons.

DELAMERE DOCK, WESTON POINT, c. 1908

This postcard shows Weston Point, where the River Weaver enters the Manchester Ship Canal. It was also close to here that Saltport was constructed and opened to traffic in September 1892. Saltport was 1892 to enable the Ship Canal Company to start to earn some revenue. Its main feature was a 700 feet-long jetty which was capable of handling vessels of up to 5,000 tons. As there was a railway link to the main line and no charges made on either imports or exports, Saltport rapidly became very popular with both importers and exporters.

WESTON POINT, c. 1904

In order to link the River Weaver with the Manchester Ship Canal, a short section of canal was built from the River Weaver to Weston Point. The river itself was allowed to enter the Ship Canal and a series of 10 sluices were built to control the flow of the water into the River Mersey. In addition, Weston Mersey Lock was constructed to allow vessels to gain access to the River Mersey. This postcard shows an artist's impression of the lock into the River Weaver and the mariners' church and lighthouse at Weston Point.

RUNCORN, c. 1928

This view shows the Ship Canal as it passes through Runcorn. It is after Runcorn that the Canal and the River Mersey separate and follow their own courses to Bollin Point, east of Warrington where the Mersey crosses the Ship Canal. It is at Runcorn, where the deepest cutting for the Ship Canal had to be made - 66 feet. Between Runcorn and Latchford, there is a section of 1.5 miles where the average depth of the cutting is around 55 feet. This postcard also clearly shows the width of the canal as well as the provision for wharves to allow vessels to unload directly into factories. The transporter bridge can just be seen on the left.

RCN.27   THE DOCKS, RUNCORN

RUNCORN DOCKS, c. 1960

Although captioned 'Runcorn Docks', this postcard shows the actual Ship Canal. In addition to the docks, which were parallel to the canal, there was also a lay-by constructed which provides a deep water berth for large ships and which also had facilities for the discharge of liquid sulphur into I.C.I's Runcorn works.

RUNCORN DOCKS, c. 1905

At Runcorn, the Bridgewater Canal originally entered the River Mersey, but this link was broken when the Manchester Ship Canal was built. Instead of travelling to Liverpool, goods which required transhipment to barges were transferred at Runcorn. The dock estate covers some 70 acres and the docks themselves can handle vessels of up to 2000 tons. This murky postcard shows vessels tied up at Alfred Dock as well as some of the large warehouses on the dock estate. Tidal dock is in the foreground.

RUNCORN PIER HEAD, c. 1909

This view of Runcorn appears to have been taken from the north bank of the Ship Canal, from Bridgewater Lock, looking towards the docks. The Bridgewater Lock is in the foreground and allowed vessels from Widnes to cross the River Mersey and gain entry to the Ship Canal without having to travel down to Eastham. The Pier is simply a jetty which forms part of the entrance to Runcorn Docks.

RUNCORN RAILWAY BRIDGE, c. 1902

At Runcorn, there are the first bridges across the Manchester Ship Canal, carrying road and rail links between Lancashire and Cheshire. This postcard shows the first bridge that is passed under which carries the main railway from London and Crewe to Liverpool. All the fixed bridges were designed to allow over 70 feet headroom for ships using the canal.

OPENED BY SIR JOHN T. BRUNNER, BART., M.P., MAY 29, 1905.

Length of Span from centre to centre of Towers, 1000 feet.
Height of Towers, 190 feet above high water level.
Height to bottom of Girders, 82 feet high water level.
Girders 18 feet deep, 35 feet apart.
Car 55 feet long, 24 feet wide, driven by electricity,
crosses in 2¼ minutes.

Widnes & Runcorn. Transporter Bridge.

Benbow Series.

RUNCORN TRANSPORTER BRIDGE, c. 1905

Adjacent to the railway bridge at Runcorn was the Runcorn-Widnes Transporter Bridge. The bridge, as can be seen from the note on the card, had a central span of 1000 feet, the towers were 100 feet high and the central girder 82 feet above water level. The car, as the transporter section was described as, measured 14 feet wide by 55 feet long and did the crossing in just over 2 minutes. It was built instead of a fixed bridge at a high level, to carry road vehicles and pedestrians from one side of the Ship Canal and River Mersey to the other. The Transporter Bridge was eventually replaced by a fixed structure when the volume of road traffic increased dramatically in the 1960s.

34

SKTH.1. THE SHIP CANAL. STOCKTON HEATH.

STOCKTON HEATH, c. 1960

After leaving Runcorn the canal passes the Randal Sluices which allow flood water to be drained into the River Mersey. The sluices are visible to those travelling along the canal, but one feature is not - the Vyrnwy Subway, which carries the pipeline carrying fresh water from Wales to Liverpool. This postcard shows a vessel heading towards Eastham as it passes Stockton Heath, close to Walton Lock and the Warrington Wharf.

TIMBER STANDS, 1933

Timber was a very important commodity which was brought in along the Manchester Ship Canal. There where several areas along the canal where timber could be unloaded. This particular timber is at Warrington, but it was typical of all other areas where timber was unloaded. The timber was used not only by the construction industry, but also in the manufacture of paper and board.

THE CANAL AT WARRINGTON, c. 1975

At Warrington, there are three swing bridges across the Manchester Ship Canal - Chester Road, Northwich Road and Knutsford Road. In addition, there is also a high level road bridge at Latchford. When the swing bridges opened to allow boats to travel along the canal, it caused serious traffic problems for Warrington and there has often been suggestions that a high level bridge should be built to take traffic. This postcard shows a vessel between the Knutsford Road and Northwich Road bridges. The Knutsford Road bridge is visible here. It weighs 1,350 tons and is 248 feet long and 36 feet wide. The bridge rests on 60 rollers which are operated by hydraulic power. Beyond the road bridge,Latchford Viaduct is visible in the background.

LATCHFORD VIADUCT, c. 1895

This view is from the opposite direction to the previous picture and shows the *Fairy Queen* – one of the regular pleasure craft which operated on the Manchester Ship Canal in the 1890s - as it leaves Latchford Lock prior to passing under Latchford Viaduct. This viaduct originally carried the London and North Western Railway's line from Manchester and Stockport to Warrington and Liverpool. The viaduct is 280 feet long with a central span of 251 feet and has a clearance of 72 feet 5 inches. Beyond it can be seen Knutsford Road Swing Bridge and, beyond that, Latchford High Level Bridge.

Latchford Locks, Manchester Ship Canal, Warrington.

LATCHFORD LOCKS, c. 1904

The first set of locks after Eastham is at Latchford, about 21 miles from Eastham. At Latchford, vessels are raised 12 feet 6 inches. As with the other locks, there are two locks at Latchford, the larger one measuring 600 feet by 65 feet and a smaller one measuring 350 feet by 45 feet. This use of parallel locks ensured that delays were kept to a minimum and that water was not wasted by using the large locks for small vessels. This postcard shows a boat and its accompanying tug at Latchford.

LATCHFORD LOCKS, c. 1908

At each set of locks, a set of sluice gates were constructed to help control the flow of water and maintain a constant depth of water. These sluices were very important as the main supply of water for the Ship Canal is the River Irwell which is liable to rapid rises in level due to heavy rain on the Pennines. The sluices at Latchford, which can be seen behind the moored vessel on the right, were capable of handling 200,000 gallons of water a minute.

THELWALL VIADUCT, 1971

With the exception of the replacement of the Runcorn-Widnes Transporter Bridge with a fixed bridge, the Manchester Ship Canal has only been bridged twice since it was completed. Travelling from Eastham to Manchester, the first of these bridges is at Thelwall, where the M6 motorway crosses the canal. Work on the Thelwall Viaduct started in 1959 and was completed in 1963. The viaduct, which is 4,427 feet long, consists of 36 arches and rises to a height of 93 feet above the water level.

WARBURTON BRIDGE

When the Manchester Ship Canal was constructed, major roads which were affected were replaced by swing bridges, but where minor roads were concerned, usually ferries were introduced. However, at Warburton, a toll bridge was erected across the canal. This bridge, shown here, rises to 74 feet above the level of the canal and to cross it, both pedestrians and motorists have to pay a toll. The construction of this bridge means that motorists do not have to travel to Barton or Warrington to cross the canal in order to travel between places like Altrincham and Irlam.

PARTINGTON COALING BASIN

Partington is the nearest point on the Manchester Ship Canal for the coalfields of Lancashire, Derbyshire and Staffordshire. As a result, special facilities were constructed to allow coal to be loaded into ships directly from railway waggons. This meant that coal could be moved directly from the collieries to the ships for either bunkering, taking around the coast to other markets or for export. Three loading shutes were provided on each side of the canal as well as special lay-bys so as ships did not obstruct the main channel.

PARTINGTON COAL TIPS, c. 1920

With the decline in coal-fired shipping, the basins at Partington were later adapted to handle chemicals and other products associated with the chemical industry, such as soda. Later still, facilities were provided here for oil storage and the handling of bulk chemicals and high and low-flash oil products. This postcard shows a vessel about to be berthed at Partington, either to bunker or collect a cargo of coal. On the left can be seen the railway lines used to bring in coal and take away chemicals and other imports handled here.

Irlam Locks

IRLAM LOCKS

Irlam locks raise the Ship Canal a further 16 feet. The locks are in close proximity to the railway bridge carrying former Cheshire Lines Committee railway between Manchester and Liverpool via Warrington. Irlam was also the location for the Lancashire Steel Corporation's works, which took advantage of the Ship Canal to bring its raw materials directly to the steel works, thereby reducing transport costs.

SLUDGE SHIP *MANCUNIUM*, 1933.

At Davyhulme, Manchester Corporation built a sewage works, which was opened in 1894. A lay-by was constructed here so that sludge boats could tie up and load treated sewage to be dumped at sea. This photograph shows the Rivers Committee on board the *Mancunium* in 1933. This vessel was specially adapted to take the sludge from Davyhulme, along the Ship Canal to dumping grounds in Liverpool Bay. The *Mancunium* was mined and sunk, without loss of life, in Liverpool Bay in 1941. This traffic only ceased in the 1980s when a pipeline was constructed to carry the sludge to Liverpool and out to sea.

BARTON HIGH LEVEL BRIDGE, 1959

In October 1960, a new crossing of the Manchester Ship Canal was completed and opened. This was at Barton and it became only the third crossing of the Canal that was not interrupted when a boat passed along. This new bridge formed part of the Stretford-Eccles bypass (M63). When opened, it was only two lanes wide in each direction but, it the late 1980s, engineers skilfully widened the carriageways to make it three lanes in each direction. This photograph shows the *Lorna* passing under the partially completed Barton High Level Bridge.

BARTON BRIDGES, c. 1930

At Barton, there are several features close together: Barton Locks where the canal is raised 15 feet, the High Level Bridge carrying the M63, Barton Road Bridge and the Barton Aqueduct carrying the Bridgewater Canal. This postcard shows the latter two features and the canal itself, which at Barton Locks is 330 feet wide.

AERIAL VIEW OF BARTON BRIDGES, c. 1950

This aerial view of Barton clearly shows both Barton Road Bridge and the Barton Aqueduct as a ship passes through. Unlike the other bridges which had to be opened, these two bridges were pivoted at their centre point so that when they open, they are parallel to the canal. Thus, at Barton, the canal is divided into two sections which allowed smaller vessels to pass under the bridges without the need for them to be swung open. In the trees in the foreground is All Saint's Barton, which was built in 1869 by the de Traffords and is, architecturally, one of the finest Catholic churches in the area. It is best seen from the canal.

BARTON BRIDGE, c. 1930

Another view of Barton Road Bridge taken from the Barton Aqueduct shows a vessel making its way upstream to Manchester. It clearly shows the tower which operates both the road bridge and aqueduct. On the south side of the canal, there is a cabin from which the men, who close the gates to stop road traffic, work.

TUG PASSING THROUGH BARTON BRIDGE, c. 1920
A view of Barton Bridge just after a large vessel has passed through on its way to Manchester. Notice the aft tug, with its paddle-wheel box construction.

BARTON BRIDGE, c. 1905

This postcard shows Barton Road Bridge looking form Barton Village towards Trafford Park. The bridge shown here replaced one which had been built in the 1740s to replace an earlier one that had been demolished to make the advance south by Bonnie Prince Charlie more difficult. The gates, which were closed when the bridge was swung, can be seen on the left of the picture, whilst in the background is All Saints Church, Barton.

BRINDLEY'S ORIGINAL BARTON AQUEDUCT

The original Barton Aqueduct was opened in 1761 and was designed to carry the Bridgewater Canal over the River Irwell. When it was completed, it was regarded as one of the wonders of the modern world and attracted visitors from many parts to marvel at it. When the Manchester Ship Canal was planned, Brindley's aqueduct had to be demolished as it did not provide adequate headroom for ships. As the present aqueduct is slightly to the east of the original one, it is still possible to see some of the stonework on Brindley's aqueduct on the north bank of the Manchester Ship Canal.

BARTON SWING AQUEDUCT, 1936

The replacement aqueduct had to be able to be swung open to allow ships to pass along the Manchester Ship Canal. In order to achieve this and, at the same time, not to have to empty and refill a section of the Bridgewater Canal, an ingenious solution was adopted. This involved creating a tank which could be sealed at both ends and sealing the ends of the canal and then swinging the tank full of water. The new aqueduct weighed 1450 tons, a method of which 800 tons was water. It is 235 feet long, 18 feet wide and 6 feet deep. This view shows the aqueduct in the open position for vessels using the Bridgewater Canal and closed to shipping of the Manchester Ship Canal. The towpath for horses was placed at a higher level than the canal, on a walkway, where the men in the photograph are standing.

54

MODE WHEEL LOCKS, MANCHESTER.

MODE WHEEL LOCKS, c. 1930

Mode Wheel Locks are the last locks on the Manchester Ship Canal. They control the level of the water in the docks at Manchester and Salford. They were built on the site of earlier locks which were used to control the flow of water when the River Irwell was used for navigation during the eighteenth and nineteenth centuries.

MODE WHEEL LOCKS, c. 1955

Looking towards the City of Manchester, this aerial view of Mode Wheel Locks shows their location in relation to the docks and Trafford Park. On the left of the canal, beyond the locks, are the Docks Number 6 to 9, whilst on the south side is Trafford Park Industrial Estate. The boat in the foreground is tied up at one of the oil termir s which were located between Mode Wheel Locks and the bridges at Barton. The dry docks are just beyond the locks, on the right-hand side of the canal.

Manchester Ship Canal.

GRAVING DOCK, c. 1905

Close to Mode Wheel Locks facilities were created for the repair of ships. A small graving dock was opened in 1894 and this was gradually enlarged as the demand for its facilities increased. This postcard shows a ship in the dry-dock at Manchester undergoing repairs; three further docks belonging to Manchester Dry Docks Co. Ltd. are out of sight to the left of the graving dock. The sluices and Mode Wheel locks are seen here from the Manchester side.

The two first Steamers to enter The New Dock. opened 13th July 1905

OPENING OF NO 9 DOCK, 13TH JULY, 1905

No 9 Dock was the last dock to be built at the Manchester end of the Canal. It was built on the site of the old Manchester Racecourse, which the Manchester Ship Canal Company had purchased for £2,562,000. The new dock took three years to complete and was officially opened by Edward VII. This postcard shows the first two steamers to enter the dock, watched by a large crowd of people. Part of the old racecourse is visible on the far bank - the grandstand providing an excellent vantage point!

NO 9 DOCK, c. 1910

No 9 dock was the largest dock at the Manchester end of the canal. When completed, it was 28 feet deep and 250 feet wide, thus enabling it to handle the very largest ships which could use the canal. This view shows No 9 dock prior to the First World War before the construction of the grain elevator which later dominated that end of this particular dock.

NO 9 DOCK, 1922

This artist's impression of No 9 Dock is taken from Trafford Wharf, looking across the Canal. In the background can be seen No 1 Elevator, which could hold 40,000 tons of grain. The grain could be unloaded directly into the elevator or, alternatively on to barges. No 2 elevator, built later, could handle the unloading of 6 vessels at any one time. Part of New Barns Junction (with the L.M. & S. Railway) is seen to the south of No 9 Dock.

NO 9 DOCK, c. 1955

Another view of No 9 Dock, looking towards the city centre and photographed somewhat later, but showing the quaysides lined with ships. Also visible are two barges making their way towards the canal proper. It is very likely that these were grain barges, having been loaded from one or other of the two grain elevators at No 9 Dock. It was claimed that 300 tons of grain could be loaded onto barges in an hour - if the grain was loose - or 50 tons (450 sacks) if it was bagged.

NO 9 DOCK AND THE *MANCHESTER EXPORTER,* c. 1966

The scene at the end of No 9 Dock as *Manchester Exporter* is unloaded and reloaded. On the right are grain barges being loaded from another ship. These barges would take the grain along the Ship Canal and the River Irwell as far as Hulme Lock from whence they would enter the Bridgewater Canal to go to Kellogg's factory in Trafford Park. The *Manchester Exporter* was built in 1952 and was acquired by Manchester Liners from the Cairn Line in 1965.

NO 9 DOCK AT NIGHT

This view shows No 9 dock at night with the ships' lights reflecting in the water - an attractive scene. However, it was not always peace and quiet at the docks during the evening. Some vessels would be worked round the clock to ensure a rapid turn-round. Manchester docks were lit by electricity from the beginning, taking advantage of this new form of lighting which was just becoming available in the 1890s.

NO 9 CONTAINER DOCK, c. 1972

During the late 1960s, new methods of conveying goods were developed - containerisation. This heralded the end for many of the traditional ways of transporting goods by sea. At Manchester, No 9 Dock was converted to handle container traffic. With its direct railway links, it was ideally placed to provide a quick transfer from land to sea transport. Here one of the Manchester Liners, the 12,040 ton *Manchester Concorde*, built in 1969, loads at No 9 Dock. In the early 1970s, this vessel was on service between Manchester and Montreal.

NO 8 DOCK, c. 1904

Until the construction of No 9 dock, the largest of the docks at Manchester was No 8, shown here looking towards Salford. In addition to the various storage sheds on this quay, there were also 13 seven-storey cotton warehouses for the import of cotton from America and other cotton-growing areas. To assist with loading and unloading cargoes, there were also derricks on the roofs of some of the sheds so that the quayside was not cluttered and road vehicles had easy access to collect their loads directly from the ship.

NO 8 DOCK, c. 1910

This is another view of No 8 Dock with the *Carib Prince* at the quayside on the right. In 1898, ships for places like the Baltic ports, Bombay, Scandinavia and America used this dock. Sailings for the more distant ports was usually at 10 days or fortnightly intervals whilst those for coastal ports and the near continent sailed weekly, or in some cases, two or three times a week.

No. 7 Dock, Manchester Ship Canal.   227.

NO 7 DOCK, c. 1908

No 7 Dock was one of the original docks intended for larger vessels travelling longer distances. As with the other docks, there were storage sheds on the quayside to facilitate loading and unloading directly in and out of covered areas. This postcard shows the *Manchester Inventor* (on the left-hand side of the illustration) moored at No 7 Dock. *Manchester Inventor* was built in 1907 and was originally the *Celtic King*. She was torpedoed and sunk off Ireland in 1917.

NO 6 DOCK, c. 1960

Until the 1970s, it was possible to see some of the ships berthed in Manchester, from Trafford Road. These ships were using No 6 Dock. It was not uncommon to have a view of the bow of a ship looming over a vehicle using the road-similar to this illustration, showing a ship berthed at one of the Salford docks. This freighter is the 9,442 ton *Pacific Northwest*, built in 1954 and owned by Furness Withy.

TRAFFORD ROAD BRIDGE, c. 1910

The last bridge across the Manchester Ship Canal is Trafford Road Bridge, linking Stretford and Salford. Like the other swing bridges it was originally worked by hydraulic power. Trafford Road Bridge has a span of 75 feet and weighs 1800 tons. When ships regularly used the canal, it had to be swung to allow vessels to reach Pomona docks (Nos 1-4). As the bridge was on a major tram route between the two towns, special provision had to be made for overhead wires to be disconnected whenever the bridge was swung. When opened for shipping, long traffic jams developed, especially during the rush hours. Eventually, it was agreed that the bridge would not be opened during the rush hours unless it was absolutely necessary.

NO 2 DOCK, c. 1908

Beyond Trafford Road Bridge there were four smaller docks, intended for use by coastal traffic, those vessels sailing to the nearer continental ports and for perishable goods. This postcard shows No 2 dock with Manchester in the background and an atmospheric smoky sky overhead.

NO 1 DOCK

Docks Nos 1 to 4 were known as Pomona Docks and were the nearest to Manchester. They were smaller than the Salford docks, but nevertheless were equally as important. Between them, these docks had 33.5 acres of water, 23 acres of quayside and 1.75 miles of quay fronting the water. This view shows both 1 and 2 docks, which have now disappeared. It should be noted that there was never a No 5 dock, although one was planned to be opposite Nos 3 and 4 docks on the Salford side of the canal.

MANCHESTER DOCKS, c. 1955

Scenes like this would have been witnessed by those using or visiting the docks in the 1950s with ships lining the quays. This is one of the docks used by vessels which would have sailed to more distant ports rather than those around the coast of the British Isles and the nearer European ports.

CANAL RAILWAYS, MANCHESTER DOCKS, c. 1912

When the docks were built, railway lines were laid on the quayside to reduce the need to handle goods that arrived or were to be dispatched by rail. This postcard clearly shows the railway lines as well as the large number of cranes that were required to achieve a rapid turn-round of ships using the docks.

LOADING A BIG GUN, MANCHESTER DOCKS, c. 1914

The opening of the docks at Manchester made the export of large loads from engineering works in and around Manchester much easier. This postcard shows a large gun barrel made by Whitworth's in Manchester arriving at the docks, drawn by a team of about 10 horses. Whitworth's factory was in Openshaw and the gun barrel would have had to cross Manchester to reach the docks.

UNLOADING BANANAS, MANCHESTER DOCKS, c. 1905

This view of Manchester docks shows stevedores unloading bananas from a recently arrived boat and loading them on railway waggons. Over the waggons can be seen the canopy of the fruit warehouse, which comprised of cool storage areas at ground level and an auction room on the first floor.

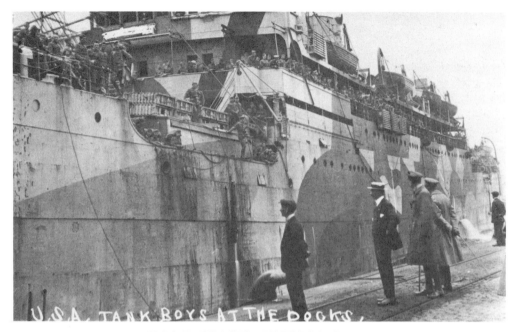

'U.S.A. TANK BOYS AT THE DOCKS', 1918

During the first world war, Manchester Docks played an important part in the war effort. Not only were raw materials and food supplies brought in through the docks, but, during 1918, American troops landed in Manchester on their way to France. This postcard shows a troop ship moored in Manchester, awaiting to disembark the soldiers. The ship's name - top left - has been scratched out by the photographer to prevent its identification by the enemy. However, according to the records, this vessel was the *City of Exeter*.

IVANHOE c. 1894

The opening of the Manchester Ship Canal provided the area with a tourist attraction - trips along the Ship Canal between Liverpool and Manchester and also from Manchester Cathedral, overlooking the River Irwell to the docks. Vessels like the *Fairy Queen* and the paddle-steamer *Ivanhoe*, - shown here approaching Latchford - were regular vessels on these trips. *Ivanhoe* was one of the vessels which came up from Liverpool for the official opening of the Canal in May 1894.

MANCHESTER PROGRESS c. 1968

Manchester Progress was one of a fleet of cargo liners which were operated by Manchester Liners of Manchester and whose names were prefixed with the name 'Manchester'. This particular vessel was built in 1967 and had a gross weight of 8,176 tons. The vessel was sold in 1971 and converted to a cellular container ship and renamed *Manchester Concept*. In 1973, she was sold to Mercantile Leasing Co, who disposed of her in 1980, when she was renamed *Cherry Bunga*. The tug is the M.S.C.*Old Trafford* and the location appears to be Irlam locks.

S.S. PHILAE, c. 1907

There were ships of all shapes and sizes using the Manchester Ship Canal. This illustration, and those following,
show some of the ships which appeared on the Manchester Ship Canal, whose visits were recorded for posterity
as postcards. This one shows the *Philae*, moored possibly in Manchester with a load of timber.

S.S. SAGAMORE, c. 1905

The illustration shows the *Sagamore* in Manchester. Again, it is not clear which dock she was tied up at or what she was carrying. This ship gives one the impression of a tanker, but it may have been carrying bulk dry cargo.

SCHOHARIE, c. 1910

This postcard shows the *Schoharie*, registered in Savannah, Georgia, in one of the locks along the Manchester Ship Canal. This vessel may have brought a load of cotton to Manchester in the years preceding the first world war.

S. S. *RAVENSWORTH*, c. 1906

The S S *Ravensworth* looks as if she has brought a load of timber into Manchester. If she was a timber carrier, she probably moored at Trafford Wharf where there were facilities to unload and store large amounts of timber. The timber probably came from the Baltic and would have been used either for constructional purposes or for the newspaper industry.

FERNMOOR, c. 1910

This view of No 9 dock is taken from a different angle from those which appear earlier in the book. It is looking from the grain elevator toward the canal and shows the *Fernmoor* in port. It must have been taken on a quiet day as the opposite side of the dock does not appear to have any shipping there.

6th Destroyer Flotilla at Manchester, June 18th, 1929

H.M.S. "Wolfhound."

HMS *WOLFHOUND*, 18TH JUNE, 1929

Although most of the vessels which visited Manchester were merchant ships, from time to time ships of the Royal Navy also visited Manchester. This postcard shows the destroyer HMS *Wolfhound*, part of the 6th Flotilla of the Atlantic Fleet, making her way along the Canal on 18th June 1929. The other destroyers which visited Manchester at the same time were HMS *Campbell*, HMS *Westcott*, HMS *Wessex* and HMS *Wakeful*. The ships tied up at Trafford Wharf and a series of events was organised for their crews.

TUG *ACTON GRANGE*, c 1910

This is another of the tugs which operated on the Manchester Ship Canal, named after one of the places the canal passed, Acton Grange. Like many of the tugs operating on the Ship Canal when this postcard was published, *Acton Grange* was a paddle tug. It was at Acton Grange where the London and North Western Railway Company had to raise their main line between London and Glasgow to enable vessels to pass along the Ship Canal.

NEREUS, c. 1954

A large ship, the *Nereus*, makes its way along the Manchester Ship Canal in the 1950s led by one of the Ship Canal Company's tugs. It is not clear where this photograph was taken, but it is very likely that it was at the Manchester end of the canal, as the vessel approached Mode Wheel Locks.

'HAVING A HEAVENLY TIME AT MANCHESTER', c. 1908

A drawing of a 'flying machine' has been added to this view of Nos 8, 7 and 6 Docks, looking towards Manchester. The Manchester Ship Canal provided Manchester with a vital and valuable life-line in the first half of the twentieth century. It brought the industrial production of a large area easier access to overseas markets and reduced the dependence of the area on the railways and especially on the Port of Liverpool, whose failure to modernise and charge reasonable rates was always a source of criticism by industrialists in other parts of the North West, especially around Manchester. Today, the journey along the Manchester Ship Canal is not as exciting as it was twenty years ago with vessels of all nations and sizes sailing to Manchester. However, there is still plenty to see and for Mancunians to be proud of the efforts of their forebears.

Also published by **S.B. Publications** in the series 'A Portrait in Old Picture Postcards':

Bootle, Vols. 1 & 2
Liverpool, Vols. 1 & 2
Rock Ferry, New Ferry & Bebington
Old Bebington
Southport

Chester, Vols. 1 & 2
Crewe, Vols. 1 & 2
The Dane Valley
The Villages of West Cheshire
Nantwich

Bury
The Bridgewater Canal
Manchester United F.C.

Aston Villa
Bournville
The Black Country, Vols. 1 & 2
Walsall and District
Wolverhampton, Vols. 1 & 2
Stourbridge and District

General Titles:
Farming Times: A Chronicle of Farming
Constabulary Duties: A History of Policing

Aberystwyth, Vols. 1 & 2

Llandudno
Snowdonia

Ruthin
Rhyl
Wrexham
Chirk & the Glyn Valley Tramway
Connah's Quay
Hawarden
Hollywell

Shrewsbury
Wellington
The Lost Villages of Telford

Pershore and District

Potteries Picture Postcards
Newcastle-under-Lyme
Staffordshire Moorlands
Mining Memories (North Staffordshire)
Stafford and District

Other titles available and in preparation. For full details write (enclosing S.A.E.) to:
S.B. Publications, c/o 19 Grove Road, Seaford, East Sussex, BN25 1TP.